NOT MY
WHITE SAVIOR

NOT MY
WHITE SAVIOR

JULAYNE LEE

a vireo book | rare rird rooks
los angeles, calif.

Demone,
For Koots to
the way! Remember
your truth
always matters! Doebs
In Peace +
t Poetry!
Julayn
Korea Center
adapted
POC workshop

THIS IS A GENUINE VIREO BOOK

A Vireo Book | Rare Bird Books
453 South Spring Street, Suite 302
Los Angeles, CA 90013
rarebirdbooks.com

Set in Minion
Printed in the United States

10 9 8 7 6 5 4 3 2 1

Publisher's Cataloging-in-Publication data is available upon request.

For adopted Koreans
and what we have lost

Contents

Introduction

The Temperature
    The Sound of My Name is Revolution
    I Am From a Revolution
    Asian American History 101
    How Often Do You Masturbate?
    Return to Sender
    The Price of Silence

More Than Salt Can Hold
    A Very Terrible Trauma
    Dear White Family,
    Relinquishment Quiz
    Consider
    Drop Box
    My Body's DMZ
    Said Child
    For My Mother
    Jealousy
    Mother's Day Mourning
    Honor Thy Father
    Birthday Surprise!
    My Last Birthday

See Out of These Slits
    Harry Holt's Little Shop of Horrors
    Fuck You, White Barbie
    Eyes Wide Open
    Racist Hair
    Spa Stories

My Body is Testimony
    100 Day American
    Dear Adopters,
    Assimilation
    Seventh Grade White Men
    Stupid Things People Say to Adopted Koreans
    Are You My Mother?
    The Map of My Body
    Cousinland
    What Language Do You Dream In?
    The Words Don't Fit in My Brain
    Homeland Insecurities
    What Do You Miss About Korea?
    After I Left
    Dual Citizen

A Holocaust of Children
    Death Should Not Inspire Me
    Open Letter to the Korean Red Cross
    KADalicious
    The Plane to France
    Pyeongchang 2018 Charter
    Korean ICA—Internment Camps of Abduction
    North of the 38th or Mr. Obama Please Apologize!
    Teleporting Babies
    Psalm for White Saviors
    My Ancestors Were Royalty

Notes

Acknowledgments

About the Author

INTRODUCTION

As a result of the Korean War, approximately two hundred thousand Koreans have been sent to Western countries via inter-country adoption (ICA). I am one of those two hundred thousand. We are living evidence of a history that has far too often been romanticized, glamorized, and inaccurately and incomprehensively documented. However, we have the grand opportunity to bear witness to the evolution of our own history.

This collection of poetry traces my journey from Korea to Minnesota to Los Angeles. Adoptees are often told how lucky we are and how grateful we should be because we have had a *better life*. Whenever I hear this, I question the definition of *better*. Better than what? Better than staying with our original families? Better than preserving our ethnic heritage? Alongside any gratitude or luck, lay a multitude of layers of complexity of grief, trauma, and loss. We are multi-dimensional, unique individuals, and each of us has a story to tell.

It is my vision that this book will challenge conventional perceptions and narratives of inter-country and transracial adoption and continue to shift the discourse to a broader spectrum, deconstructing the white savior mentality. This is my contribution to the documentation of our invisible history.

Thank you for joining me on this journey.
Julayne

I.

The Temperature

The Sound of My Name is Revolution

My name tastes like a princess torte
from Wuollet's, the Larchmont Bungalow
it's savory like Thai Cambodian lunch
at Sophy's in Long Beach
it's like Brie cheese
paired with Penfold's Cabernet
refreshing, healthy
like pressed raw juice

My name is where I start
when, where, how did I begin?
my personal history
basic human right
yet systems, governments
block me

Is it privilege to know these things?
is it privilege
to have only one legal name
on this planet
instead of three?
is it privilege to have a name
you can just say
no one reacts to?
sometimes I can't even just say
my name to an operator

My name a blessed curse
I will take to the grave
unless I hire an attorney
stand before a judge
bring two trusted witnesses
pay four hundred dollars
notify the INS
initiate a background check
on myself

So I embrace each secret part of my name

the sound of my name is revolution
a melody
unknown, familiar song
people mispronounce
like fingernails on chalkboards
when I see my name misspelled
it invokes trauma
it's revolting, repulsive
a punch to my gut

My name paints every shade of blue
like the ocean
a palette of reactions
water can be friend or foe
bring relief or tragedy
quenches thirst at marathon's end
chokes out life in a New Orleans hurricane

My name *Julayne*
means *youthful heart, youthful spirit*

perfect love sometimes absent
I found the missing piece
for my heart-shaped name

I measure my name in metric and imperial
measure it in wine, cheese, olives, hummus,
chocolate, red velvet cupcakes,
measure it in maple bacon sweet potato fries,
steak salads,
and ice cream birthday cakes

The temperature of my name a fever
when too many people I meet
for the first time
respond in introduction
that I have such a beautiful name
or icy cold
just because you think my name is beautiful
I've never heard that name before!
doesn't mean I want to have coffee with you
to talk about how exotic and romantic
you think it sounds

The texture of my name like a nail file
one side sand paper
few accurately pronounce
and not project awkwardness
the first time
the other side smooth,
beautiful,
easy to pronounce
rhymes with Tulane
rolls off your tongue like a revolutionary chant

Ann Taylor destination the scent of my name
extinct fragrance
my name is Ocean Breeze
Eucalyptus, Jasmine

If I could give my name a new meaning
you'd hear
Ambitious
Relentless
Rainmaker
Fierce
Genuine
Loyal
Badass!

I Am From a Revolution

That won't let memory die
I swam in peace and war
submerged trauma
in my mother's womb
sold to white savior body snatchers

I am from a revolution
that floats in Pacific oxygen
waves rock eternal slumber
exhale between east and west
mask grief, loss

I am from a revolution
that rests in Buddhist temples
meditates on kimchi
drinks beer and soju with monks
revolution that conquered Japan
revolution that will conquer
star-spangled banner freedom
which revolution are you from?

Asian American History 101

This class didn't exist in my day
we were invisible
liberal arts degree failed
to educate me about myself
chorus member in *The King & I*
white people in yellow face
no grad school Asian American History
Minnesota's oldest university
I pieced together my own
Asian American History course

In Minnesota
I signed up for night school
weekend class on Washington
Equilibrium
Diaspora Flow
Asian American Renaissance
at The Loft
Macalester Chapel
Weisman on the East Bank
Theater Mu
Mixed Blood Theater
on the West Bank

Distance learning
at the Hot House in Chicago

East Meets West in Boston
for The Summit
travel through a dozen Asian countries
The House of Sharing
weekly demonstration
with the Comfort Women

In Cali, my weekend class
Sunday Jump on Temple
Common Ground night school
Café on Tuesday Night
The Great Mic
and Our Mic
because We Own the 8th

My professors have PhDs in their
Asian American experience
I Was Born With 2 Tongues
Isangmahal
Proletariat Bronze
Mongrel
Mango Tribe
Magnetic North
Blue Scholars
Yellow Rage
ForWord
Ishle Park
Bao Phi
Giles Li
Ed Bok Lee
Anida Yeou Ali
Theresa Vu

Beau Sia
Lady Basco
Traci Kato-Kiriyama
Denizen Kane
David Mura
Joe Kadi
Lawson Inada

They assigned me
five-dollar chapbooks
CDs, documentaries
Bamboo Among the Oaks
Yellow: Race in America Beyond Black and White
Asian American Dreams
Angry Asian Man
First Person Plural
Resilience
Broken Speak
Legends from Camp
Song I Sing
extra credit?
move to Korea
agitate as an activist
incite a revolution
fundraise for the Summit
continue our education
write and share publicly
workshop with Asian American youth
document our history
with poetry and pictures

The tuition affordable
No student loans
No work study program
five–ten dollar sliding scale per class
or FREE!

Pop-up classrooms
each life a library of lessons
poetry and art
write our history
for the next generation!

How Often Do You Masturbate?

Inspired by "Not Your Fetish" by I Was Born With Two Tongues

I did not ask, *Do you masturbate?*
I asked *how often?*
now before you start blushing
and try to deny any private behavior
and get in your one-track mind
let me clarify
how often
do you masturbate
in my culture?
Korean culture?
Oh, see now
the answer is even more embarrassing
but you're more willing to admit
that you unconsciously masturbate
in my culture regularly
some of you daily
some of you
it's easier to identify how often you don't masturbate
in my culture

Koreatown
Korean dramas
Kpop

Korean Wave
KCON
Kakao Talk
Kogi trucks
and kimchi
make you more hipster and trendy than your neighbors who
shop at the farmers market
don't own cars
have one of those toilets you don't flush

Living in Koreatown
does not mean you're more socially conscious
it means you masturbate not only in my culture
but also Mexican culture
having a premium membership to Drama Fever
so you can watch Korean dramas commercial free
only means
you can watch Korean dramas
commercial free
adding kimchi to your menu
does not make your New American restaurant
diverse and cultured
especially when your kimchi sucks

You think teaching English in Korea for a year
makes you an expert on all things Korean
but remember
Koreans were exploiting you
as their English prostitute

For you
my culture is your playground

your Disneyland
for me
it means forced liberation from myself
my culture has required me to decolonize myself
my culture has asked me if I am Korean
or American
I am 100 percent both

You
get to choose
for me
this culture is my obligation
so please
stop masturbating
in my culture!

Return to Sender

Since 1953, Korea has sent over one hundred fifty thousand children to the USA via inter-country adoption. Due to a loophole in the Child Citizenship Act, there are an estimated thirty-five thousand inter-country adoptees living without US citizenship. Some have been deported to their country of origin.

Korea exported me to America
before I could speak my name
Minnesota, Land of ten thousand Lakes
Better Life, education

Forever family bruises
denied me US citizenship
homeless, absent high school degree
starvation shoplifts
military time served
America's Promised Prison Land

Deported back to Korea
Incheon Airport lobby
solitary confinement persists
no *Welcome* sign
not even a환영합니다

family reunions surround me
mother's bouquet
embraces graduated daughter

No arms encircle my ghost body

Korean streets handcuff
my life sentence
birth land homesickness
leftover kimchi barely sustains
midnight Han River bridges
protect my frozen soul
brain resists foreign language
들어오세요
throat chokes syllables
language is life
도움말

Let me survive
my lifeless sentence

The Price of Silence

We were told to never talk
about trauma that suffocates
chokes the womb
if we spoke
gratitude would silence us
grief reveal expunged lies
deceit meant to kill
force another breath
lies dance across bastard reality
governments would tumble

We were told to never talk
about lost but not found names
so our Korean families
could forget our tiny feet
our 2:00 a.m. infant cry
first Korean lullaby babble
wobbly steps, cling to furniture
one hundred–day celebration
first birthday
never worn child size hanboks
blank university entrance exams
unserved military service
first dates, soju shots
school field trips
eyelids never double folded

3:00 a.m. Kakao messages
wedding hall matrimony

We were told to never talk
about our grief and loss
more massive than Gwanghwamun
jigsaw families
framed with missing pieces
our silence bleeds a slow death

II.

More Than Salt Can Hold

A Very Terrible Trauma

for Jade

To us a victor!
to your adopters
an eternal burden
denied due process
parental needs eclipsed yours

Dutch parents dissatisfied
return policy expired
store credit refused
adult exception
diplomat father
inhabited Hong Kong

open market bought your salvation
secret money back guarantee
parents reviled
you beloved

your abandoned legacy
orphaned testament
seven-year-old Korean girl

Dear White Family,

you say you love me but you voted for hate
I cannot meet you on your white side
white lies suffocated me
I believed
I could never be white enough for you
you helped create this
to call me daughter, sister
dismantle your whiteness

Dear White Family,
do you really think you're better than me?
you said I was the most beautiful
is it inferiority oppression?
I was never white enough
Right enough
Perfect enough

Why don't you march around Jericho
until your white privilege walls
are made of justice, equality for all?

Dear White Family,
please say you regret your vote for hate
I will never be white like you
nor do I want to be

Relinquishment Quiz

Please select the answer that best matches your adoption file. If there is a match, you will get to meet your Korean mother. You have five minutes to complete the quiz.

A. Your mother was a college student
    needed to finish school
    loved you so much
    she sent you away

B. Your mother was a factory worker
    no sex education, birth control
    needed to work
    money was tight
    at least she didn't abort you

C. Your mother was a drug addict, poor
    no family, no social status, no power
    no privilege, mental illness haunted her
    I pray she got saved
    now Christian

D. Your mother was unwed
    mistress, victim, prostitute
    abandoned you at the police box

*If you fail this Relinquishment Quiz, you may try again next summer if an agency worker is available. Please schedule your quiz appointment at least two months in advance. You will need to pay the fifty-dollar fee again. We accept cash only.

Consider

after Scott Cohen, "Popular Turf Varieties"

When choosing the best variety of children
first select one
that will best suit the needs
of your whole family
that will thrive in your local environment

The most important factor to consider
in selecting
is the ability of the children to survive
the intended use from adults
is there adequate sunlight to support?
space that favors intolerant varieties of children?

Consider your choices, conditions
to plant children
installed
for an instant family.

Drop Box

Good Morning Korean Families!
If you're done with your babies
you can deposit them in the Baby Box!
Yes, that's correct.
just drop them off
no questions asked
anonymity guaranteed
a minister will care for your child
along with one hundred previously deposited children
all in the name of God and Jesus Christ!

Please consider a donation
so we can build more Baby Boxes
one on every street corner in Korea!
so all families will have this option
to deposit their unwanted children
then we'll have no unwanted children
because they're all wanted
by good church going Koreans!

You see, it's God's will to separate families
so we can perform our Christian service!
Caring for orphans in their distress!
Please dig a little deeper
give a little more
so we can build Baby Boxes
from sea to shining sea!

My Body's DMZ

Abducted, kidnapped bastard
my body split by war
breathes DMZ trauma
bleeds myth story
my body floats
between east and west
ocean salt drowned me
before I reached
Amerikkka's white supremacy shores
my unknown body
perpetually ten months old
Korean history
lied to my Buddhist soul

My birthplace straddles
US military oppression
borders liberation
divides unification
Japanese occupation
Chinese migration
Shenyang enclave
Dalian hideouts

Waldorf Astoria concierge
glares bastard judgement
white linen five course tuxedo

silverware, water goblets
outnumber my hands
Beverly Hills Wilshire Korean privilege
won't seat me

My body trafficked war crime
discarded my white name
Asian brothers court side
reclaimed my heritage
body pieces
find peace

Said Child

Guardian Kwan Soo Kim
I am not Said Child
I am your worst nightmare
I have spent more time with my adoption file
than you took to assign my random name
I know it ain't all fact
so which parts are fiction?

Did my Korean family approve you
to write my Child's Progress Report
or is it the unauthorized account
of my first ten months?

By virtue of your right as my legal guardian
you've proven you have no character
you have no integrity
you thought white people
could raise me better than Koreans
you must hate yourself more than I ever will

You will be irrevocably terminated
you and the rest of your adoption cronies
selling Korean babies
to white christian adopters

Yesterday I broke out with diarrhea
began to snivel with a cold

I hope my feces and mucus
left eternal skid marks, stains
on your reputation and conscience

My left thigh bean-size mole
you call a defect
disappeared
Did you know white American doctors
would remove it?
tamper with crime scene evidence?
you are the defect
not me!

Last night I began to vomit
accompanied with slight fever
you too would be ill
if torn from your family
subjected to trauma against your will
your recommendation: milk or rice cereal
what about my Korean mother's breast milk?
why did you deprive me?

You say I'm too young to mingle with children
how the fuck would you know?
did you ever bother to ask me?
you are too old for a relationship with the world

You signed me away
at the American Embassy in Seoul
you must have been in bed
with the Vice Consul
how is John P. Leonard doing?

remember
the US embassy
is Japan's continued colonization.

You certified a full, true, and correct copy
of my Original Family Register
but its full of No Records
false as Satan
how do you sleep at night Guardian Kim?

For My Mother

That title is not correct
this is a poem for my mothers
My first mother
Korean
gave birth to me
in the Land of the Morning Calm
My second mother
Korean
cared for me
from the orphanage to the plane
My third mother
White
abducted, bought, adopted me
raised me in the Promised Land
Three mothers
One child
One daughter

To my Korean mother
I don't know who you are
I don't know your name
I don't know your face, your history,
family, interests, home,
how you conceived me
yes, I know how babies are made but
I don't know if you were someone's wife,

someone's mistress,
someone's victim
when I was conceived
I don't know if I was your only child
sent away from our divided country
I don't know if you understand
how your choices impacted my life
I don't know if you're even alive anymore
I don't know if you think about me
but I know I think about you
I know you look like me
or should I say
I look like you
but which parts of this body you gave me
belong to you?

To my foster mother
Ahn-Soon Lim
I waited over three decades
seven thousand miles to know your name
maybe you're now in your seventies if you're still alive
Does not recognize her foster mother.
Recognizing the foster mother.
Will look for her own foster mother.
Says "mom" now and then.
This is what my adoption file says,
but what do you say?
we know the papers lie
but we don't know when

To my white mother
Mother

I'm not sure why I have to use this term when addressing you
so I have abandoned it
a purchase agreement and a
promise to raise a child in the Christian faith
do not require me to address a woman twice my age
who looks nothing like me by this title
therefore, I don't
I've been told I need to be thankful to you
for giving me a better life
rescuing me from the war-ravaged country of Korea
here is what I have to be thankful for
when you told me
you paid a lot of money for me
when you told me
if you hadn't adopted me
I'd be living a life of prostitution
on the streets of Korea
I'd be homeless or dead.
Did it ever occur to you
I can do all of those things in America?
I can go back to Korea and fulfill this destiny
or all of the above?

I'm told I should be thankful
for everything you've taught me
you taught me that control,
manipulation, brainwashing, and
spiritual abuse are normal in childrearing
that I am responsible for how you feel and look
that when we die we go to heaven
but the only way to get there

is to do the right thing
but no matter what I did
it would never
be good
enough

you taught me
that I was responsible for how God felt
that God was a white man
that it is best to be white
or at least an honorary white
but it's good to have at least one black friend
as long as he is married to a white woman
you taught me interracial marriages aren't always okay
that I should be ashamed of my body
that I am not beautiful
that college was my only option after high school
actually, you taught me a Christian college
was my only option
because I would marry someone I would meet there
you taught me that as a woman
my success would be measured by the man I would
marry and children I would birth
that it wouldn't be right to
marry someone outside of your faith
that the only political choice
was to be a pro-life Republican
you taught me that being narrow-minded,
self-righteous and judgmental are normal
you taught me that it is okay for you
to be a hypocrite
but not for me

so for all these things I cannot
and will not
be thankful

To my Korean mother
you had no choice, no power
To my foster mother
a surrogate
To my white mother
you had choice, power, privilege
and you chose to abuse it.
Three mothers.
One daughter.
who traveled this journey
alone.

Jealousy

We cannot let those people who do not love us
determine who we are.
—Nikki Giovanni

In the backyard
under giant tree shade
leaves fall
welcome winter
leaves I raked for years

Today is not for raking
but raking me over coals
my identity interrogated
my journey on trial
forced assimilation
my white parents sit in patio furniture they can't afford
demand reports of my first return to Korea

Then
my white mother
slams me to my past
Jealous I was so cute, pretty
Jealous of my skinny frame
Jealousy drips off her words
Venom throws daggers I dodge
shock me back to my childhood

past crumbles
maternal love conditional, rationed
my existence threatened her
child controlled parent
my power unaware
just wanted to make A Honor Roll
come home
sleep under safe roof
jealous of my talents you encouraged
ten year piano lessons
state competitions
inferior red second-place ribbons
coveted blue first-place ribbons
You made me into something
you could despise
resent.
Jealousy let me believe
I was the ugliest child
ever born
now you tell me
with seething envy
I was the most beautiful
in our family
but I never felt that way
I didn't belong

Raked leaves bear witness to frozen emotions
eternally jealous of your imported child
disgraceful
You
should be ashamed

still jealous of me
I
will never
be jealous
of you.

Mother's Day Mourning

Grieving
Healing
Day filled with sorrows
more than salt can hold
abandoned children grieve
now grown ass adults
grief floods hearts
like hurricanes

Lives lost,
Erased,
Invisible,
Silenced,
Deported,
Terminated.

Now parents, grandparents
we are treated like children
nation's doors slam adopted faces
own your shame

Street corners block family reunions
corrupt agencies
aunts, grandmothers
skin holds lies
secrets whisper decades' betrayal

Hallmark, FTD, boutique shops proclaim
Where Mother's Day Wishes Come True
but it's
a fucking
lie

Deception extinguishes
birthday candle wishes
Mother's Day our social media detox
try
to survive
this fucking day

Reunions kept family secrets
holiday gathering invites lost
told to end rendezvous
you deny you ever knew us
rejection once wasn't enough
we wish
we never looked for you
you wish
the same

Honor Thy Father

Honor Myself
my past
my future
well-being prays silence
self-esteem breathes mindfulness
heals sorrow filled spirit
Father's Day honors me

I was never equal to men
shall I honor you for this myth
disrespecting women
women I disrespect

fathers not exempt
titles demand respect
mixed entitlement bag
Father's Day greetings
Honor Myself

Birthday Surprise!

Happy Birthday!
Birth Days not always Happy
real, make believe, mystery?
dates edited
fabricated
infant supply chain
birth switch
Seoul orphanage
Kimpo plane
Yonsei hospital
agency files

celebrate wrong birthdays
wrong month
wrong year

Agency, hospital workers
altered infant lives
let's delete your birthdays!

Emerald birthstone wrong
April diamond exchange?
Taurus sign fake
Rooster year wrong
lunar calendar rotation
doorstep abandonment

Adoptee *Happy Birthday* needs permission
social media removed birthday
No birth certificate
No family registry

instead
Unhappy Birthday
Mystery Birthday
Unknown Birthday
Sad Birthday
Mournful Birthday
Confusing Birthday
Annoying Birthday
Frustrating Birthday
Wrong Birthday
Lied to Me About My Birthday!

Our only birthday wish
to know
which day
to celebrate…

My Last Birthday

On my last birthday
I took the 6:30 a.m. Catalina Express
Long Beach to Avalon
wind fluttered
pinned birthday ribbon
indulged free birthday coffee,
free birthday ice cream,
free birthday dinner!
Strangers offered rides
first journal entry in forever
awaited friend's arrival
late Orange County ferry
paddled with stingrays, sea lions
abandoned life jacket fished Pacific waves
tourist T-shirts, magnets, postcards
hiked Wrigley Memorial
last sunset ferry
no boyfriend birthday wishes
grieved expected behavior
thoughts of countless lives
lost on a ferry
an ocean away
many still missing
Sewol casket filled with grief

On my last birthday
I smoked a Cuban cigar in Old Havana
washed down with Cuban rum
lived my fantasy
riding shotgun in a convertible
big sunglasses
hair tied down
pink silk scarf ala Jackie O.
bartered our driver to twelve dollars
we cruised along the Melacon
backseat photo shoot
in a pink
Hello Kitty taxi!
seaside dinner our destination
our last night in Havana
capped off by Manny Pacquiao's loss
and a room full of deflated Filipinos

On my last birthday
I woke before dawn
boarded the first Oakland to LAX flight
I sat naked
in a Koreatown spa
surrounded by women
all sizes, colors
wrinkles hide millennials of secrets
what secrets live in my mother's skin?
ajumma in black lace underwear
sandpaper scrubbed my body
I sat alone on the rooftop
eating mandu rice cake soup

On my last birthday
I hope to know when my birthday is
I hope I've left a legacy
longer than a marathon
up to the heavens
On my last birthday
this is my wish.

III.

See Out of These Slits

Harry Holt's Little Shop of Horrors

*In memory of the Sueppel children: Ethan (10), Seth (7),
Mira (5), Eleanor (3)*

Dried blood cradles four
bruises caress tiny arms, feet
toddler fists scream fear
heads hit blunt force
child torsos tear apart futures
death consumes Iowa home

Harry Holt's Little Shop of Horrors
sold four babies to white-collar murder
suicide note smells concrete crash

Murdered headlines
rippled global shockwaves
Korean mothers' eternal empty arms
Harry's non-apology nauseates

Better Life failed
white savior father murder hands
your lives testify corruption
your deaths forever stain adoption

Harry sleeps in peace
six feet under
your white savior
couldn't save you

Fuck You, White Barbie

White Barbie did not help my self-esteem
she deceived me into thinking I had status
I needed
Korean Barbie
my other Korean dolls
to tell me the truth
that I am beautiful

I wish my dolls had looked like me
not blonde, white
Barbie was banned from my home
until a school friend brought her to my birthday party
excited to finally own this coveted toy
I now feared repercussions
for having Barbie
worse yet, have her taken away
she meant status

Years later
white Barbie moved on
to her white sorority sisters
too good for me
my white sister-in-law gave me
Korean Barbie
complete with doll stand
collector's box
traditional Korean clothing

My Korean dolls
destined for the shelf
not allowed to play with them
dusted them each week
began to resent them
they created work
prevented me from playing
with white Barbie

Korean Barbie would have been my friend
her destiny the shelf
in her collector's box
with her stand
clearly meant only for display
Dolls of color silenced once again

The status I thought white Barbie gave me
was a setup, false hope
smoke screen
that I could be like the cool white kids
I'd never have their status, privilege
her plan from the start
white Barbie betrayed me
when she moved into my toy box

Korean Barbie oppressed
confined by white Barbie's empire
not allowed to speak the truth.
If she did
Korean Barbie sales
would exceed white Barbie sales
how does white Barbie have so much fucking power?

Eyes Wide Open

You may want to take another photo
Someone's eyes were closed

Your camera made a racial slur
Please delete!

Almond shaped eyes are eyes wide open
digest racism
you think our eyes closed
we see everything

Cameras made for white people
with racist lens
use white filter
to see beauty, perfection

White grandmother asks
how I can see out of these slits
I see just fine
I have 20/20 vision
passed every eye exam
for over four decades

Last summer
my eyes tired
my Vietnamese optometrist
asked me to open my eyes wider

I knew he wasn't racist
like the camera
like my white grandmother

If you tell me to open my eyes
you need to do the same
you need to see true beauty

Racist Hair

My hair is racist
ain't no white person
cutting my hair
not after I waited over three decades
for a haircut that made sense
years of bad home perms
white people think Asian hair
the same as white hair

The best haircut ever
awaited me across the Pacific
down a cobblestone Seoul alley
near the women's university
ten dollars, a stylist, two assistants
topped off with a coupon
for my next visit
a salon where children get their hair colored
cuz it's what you do in Korea!

Once I crossed the line
from white to yellow
I never let another white person
touch my hair
didn't care if the white intern
felt bad when I told her *Hands off.*

I've done my time with bad haircuts
why pay someone
if I know they're going to mess it up?
Again?

Spa Stories

I.

Exfoliation grates my skin
grime like dirty rice
peppers pink plastic
hugs the massage bed
ajumma in black lace bra, panty set
tells me in Korean
to lie face down
I didn't learn that phrase
she files my skin like sandpaper
I lost a pound of dirt
scrubs my naked body
she guesses my age
each wrinkle and fold
reveals time
I sit in every tub
hot, warm, cold
every steam room
every sauna
oak, salt, clay, jade, ice

II.

My first Korean jimjilbang visit
included nudity
not mine
a random ajussi
post-World Cup match
lights turned low
he took his place on the mat
naked
stared in shock amongst shadows
nervous giggles crowded the room

IV.

My Body is Testimony

100 Day American

In memory of Madoc Hyunsu O'Callahan, Rest In Power,
February 3, 2014

American three months
death at your white father's hands
high-ranking NSA agent
your white savior abuser pleads guilty
twenty-year sentence
eight years subtracted
dishonors your brief life
your missed lifetime
your murderer serves a brief refrain
your body bruised, beaten
hurled against walls
fractured your toddler skull
bleeding brain
hemorrhaging eyes
bath time turned tragic
another Harry Holt casualty
your white savior's body
protected by prison guards
protected by PTSD

protected by mental illness
protected by psychotropic meds
false drug tests

We guard your grave
your body buried
beneath cheap plastic tombstone
your death not in vain
you'll not be forgotten
our baby brother
we'll see you soon

Dear adopters,

you don't need to be white
to be a white savior
you are not entitled
to my free labor
to teach you
adopter best practices
recipe to raise your imported child

$30,000 for your ornamental baby
left you cold broke
you plead for my handout advice
why didn't you budget for adopter training?

don't occupy my emotional space
hanboks and kimchi
do not qualify you Korean American
did you really think on the job training
enough
with babies for sale?

ASSIMILATION

Asians imitated caucAsians
Selected from photographs were we
Scandinavians dominated their adopted Asians
Isolation in my own family
Minnesota—Land of ten thousand adopted Koreans
I am not part norwegian
Lee Eun Jin is who I am
After being raised a Republican I have recovered
Three times on Sundays we went to church
Individualization was taboo
Oslo is the birthplace of my grandfather
Naturalization transformed both him and me

Seventh Grade White Men

Konichiwa! Konichiwa! Am I in Japan? No. I am in a seventh grade American classroom in Coon Rapids, Minnesota.

On what should be an ordinary day of substitute teaching in White Suburbia, USA, I am repeatedly greeted in Japanese by seventh grade whiteys. Seems they recently had a guest teacher who was, yes, Japanese. Guess they forgot the part about "appropriate use of non-English greetings." As I begin my interrogation of these ignorant white boys, it turns out they don't even know what *Konichiwa* means. I phone the cultural liaison and report their ignorant behavior.

Anyeonghaseoyo! No. I'm not in Korea when the white man greets me in perfectly pronounced Korean.

I'm still in Minnesota, in the city, not the suburbs. He claims he said this because I am carrying a bag that reads *Korea* compliments of the Korea Tourism Organization. I confront him about his ignorance and he tells me he does business with Koreans, his wife is Korean. Little does he know this is not helping his case. When I tell him I'm offended he starts to tell me he is offended, too. I walk away and tell him it's best he keep his mouth shut.

Sin chow! Nyobzoo! Still in Minnesota I want to ignore the white stranger who thinks it's his right to practice his Asian language skills on me, but instead I confront and educate the fool.

His disclaimer? There are so many children in the community who really appreciate it when he speaks to them in their first language and he has made such an effort to really understand their experience by studying their languages. Check—I'm not a child. Check—I don't speak any Asian languages.

Hanguk saram? Los Angeles white men are no different. I sit in his LinkedIn workshop and turn to the black woman next to me to confirm what I just heard. She says she thinks he's trying to show off. When I confront him, he admits he wanted to practice his Korean. And you guessed it, he has a long-time Korean friend. I give him a low score on the workshop evaluation.

Seventh grade white men, if you can't translate my face, use the language of your ancestors not mine!

Stupid Things People Say to Adopted Koreans

1. Have you met your *real* parents?

2. Why don't you speak Korean?

3. I taught English in Korea and met a Korean adoptee.

4. I adopted my daughter/son from Korea!

5. My dad served in the Korean War.

6. Are you from the North or the South?

7. Why don't you like kimchi?

8. You don't look Korean.

9. You should really watch *The Joy Luck Club*.

10. I know a Korean adoptee who met their birth mom through one of those reunion shows on Korean TV. Have you tried that?

11. Have you dated your brother? You're not biologically related so…

12. You're lucky you were adopted. At least you didn't have to grow up in an orphanage.

13. Why haven't you searched for your birth family?

14. Why haven't you gone back to Korea?

15. You know, I'm second generation Korean American and we have so much in common.

16. My partner and I are planning to adopt. Any advice?

17. Are you 100 percent Korean?

18. You should be thankful you got to go to America.

19. How long have you been studying English?

20. Are you an exchange student?

21. If you hadn't been adopted, I never would have met you!

22. Maybe it's not God's will for you to meet your Korean family.

Are You My Mother?

You demand my subway seat
because you are the elder
I stand to face you
notice familiar features
why do you look away?
do you recognize our resemblance?
can't face your guilt?

You heckle me in Namdaemun market
your kimchi the best
recipe handed down for generations
it lives only in your heart
your nose curves like mine
you move on
customers wait ten deep

Your soju smile greets me
bow as I enter your Sinchon restaurant
laugh at my survival Korean
nod as I point to steaming dishes
on nearby tables
tear up as you watch
another adoptee television reunion
remember your sent away children

You ask if I'm Japanese
as I browse your Insadong gift shop

I ask in Korean
if you are Japanese
I tell you I'm adopted
discomfort traces your face
you bear the guilt
of an entire nation

We enter your Koreatown tofu shop
you ask *How many?* in Korean
switch to English
when you hear us speak
you assume I'm kyopo
I explain I was adopted
Aigu is all you can say
hand me a menu
walk away

The Map of My Body

Feet, what do I need you for
when I have wings to fly?
—Frida Kahlo

On the map of my body
live colonial scars
seared into memory by war
carried into the next millennium
by discarded children
to cities of my unknown history

Marked for abandonment in Daejeon
wounds pierced me while in the womb
wounds that would not heal
as my body traveled north to Seoul
passed through the Pacific

Returned to the nation that gifted me these scars
I bare them to Korean media, taxi drivers, ministers
the scent of magnolias, cherry blossoms
soothe my pain
like a sauna
on a cold, wintry day

Korea marked my inner thigh
with the only clue on this treasure map

twenty stiches crisscross my face
glass slices fingers, arms

Each unknown step
in this occupied territory
Lifts me to flight
Across the Han River
Down to Cheju Island
to the top of Halla Mountain

My body is testimony to an erased history
history banned from museums
Absent from textbooks
Unknown to a new generation

A history we imprint on this nation that sent us away
a sealed tattoo longer than the Olympic Bridge
Higher than the 63 Building
Older than Confucianism

Every citizen sent away
Another missing chapter
Another wound on my body
Another stain on this nation's history.

Cousinland

thank you Eric S. for this word in the Koroot kitchen

Far, far away
somewhere East of East
sits the Korean peninsula
Land of the Morning Calm
airfare exceeds my bank account
this is not my motherland
this is my Cousinland

Familiar airport lobby stranger greets me
holds my English scrawled name
the welcome I've always wanted
tonight I want to run away
pretend I don't see him
this is my Cousinland

Who are these adopted Koreans?
Asian, black hair, almond-shaped eyes
English speakers
Australian, European, US passports
we sound not how we look

How do I eat this food I can't pronounce?
fried egg tops rice
hot stone pot holds vegetables

red chili paste decorates
like cake icing
foreign spicy taste

What is this unshapely dress?
lost beauty, tradition
how to wear a hanbok?
tie the otkorum?
how do I pronounce *otkurum*?
this is my Cousinland

June humidity begs summer apparel
Korean society won't tolerate
my sleeveless dress
women's beauty shamed

Olympics, World Cup
provide survival English
language of origin expected
impossible to my tongue, ears
heart blocks vocabulary
alphabet haunts

Why is your last name *Smith*?
Are you married?
Are you Japanese?
Why don't you speak Korean?
Are you kyopo?
Are you an original Korean?
Are you Chinese?
Why don't you speak Korean?
This is my Cousinland!

What Language Do You Dream In?

Do you dream in a language you know?
a language you're expected to know?
or is that a nightmare?

This language's silence
prohibits dream translation
into syllables of reality
dreams conjugate nightmares
where language tortures
oppresses, belittles
language takes life
deletes breath
silences you
powerless child

Language is music
you lack fluency
in this mother tongue
music is noise
clanging symbols
midnight car alarms

Cousin tongue
imbalances music library
cousin language of origin
silenced three decades strong

tongue eternally trips
over instinctive sounds
unless you wake up
from this eternal nightmare

The Words Don't Fit in My Brain

The Words Don't Fit in My Mouth
—Jessica Care Moore

Language feels like sandpaper skin
sounds like chalkboard fingernails
tastes like moldy whole grain vinegar-soaked bread
stale soju
smells like New Year's Eve Times Square

First language I knew
heard from my mother's womb
subway conversations eavesdropped
students' gossip
hear doctors, agency workers
coerce my relinquishment

Forever lost language
white colonizers stole
unfound hide and seek
literary maze
dumbfounded mother tongue

Subtitles evaporate
Korean dramas overtime
rewind, repeat bad translation
glimpse body language

forced to watch bad
Korean movies
each film
one syllable closer
to fluency

Fifteen years tutored
language partners exchange
more English
than Korean
Level 1 stuck
Return to Start
my body tries to speak
words my brain cannot
language snatched,
choked from my life
lost luggage left
at Kimpo airport

The words don't fit in my brain
like A4 paper
won't fit in letter-size folders
my life lost in translation
twisted tongue
trips over Korean alphabet
the words don't fit in my brain
but they fit in my heart

Homeland Insecurities

어디가? he asks in French-accented Korean
I reply, unsure if I've answered his question
Where are you going?
I'm going home
I'm going to Haebangchon to my third-story,
five hundred–square-foot apartment
it's where I sleep, receive my mail, store three, overweight
pieces of luggage
how can I feel at home when I am harassed by every dick-tot-
ing non-Korean I pass on the street?
if it isn't me they're harassing it's another Korean
the difference?
these assholes
understand my back-lashing tongue
defend in angry, fluent English
I tell them to go back to where they came from
this is not my home
this neighborhood which is likened to a ghetto
or the projects
no. these words are too kind
slum? no
cesspool?
yes, I live in a cesspool

어디가?

I'm going to America
Minnesota
this is where I grew up
hold citizenship
registered to vote
own property
received my passport
the Land of ten thousand Adopted Koreans!
I should feel at home
a multitude of Asian faces
yet our paths rarely crossed
my childhood home
surrounded on three sides
by farm fields
it is here I'm told
to go back to where I came from
explains my urge
to run away from home
I want to run
to something that feels like home
America is not my home

Living in Korea
I did not feel like I belong in America more
nor like I belong in Korea more
it only made me feel
that I belong everywhere
less
as I begin to explain this
he barely lets me finish
by stating he too

feels the same
he understands
I don't need to explain

Where is home for you?
how could Korea be my homeland
when I couldn't even find it on a map?
North Korea? South Korea?
what about West and East Korea?

Where is home for you?
instead of sounding
like a list of place names
memorized for a junior high geography quiz
her reply sounds more like a melody
Home is wherever my sisters are
wherever my sisters are

Home is wherever my two hundred thousand
Korean brothers and sisters
are scattered around the globe
three continents
thirty countries

Home is in Amsterdam
we stroll canals
Van Gogh museum
Red Light district

Home is in Copenhagen
I meet a Norwegian brother and sister
we drink ourselves silly
dance and sing karaoke

until we are kicked out
of the smoky, dimly lit bar

Home is in Oslo
Norwegian folk village tour
browse local pop music scene,
end our day
at the only Korean restaurant
in the city

Home is in London
you dodge bombs on buses
we wait to hear *I'm okay*

Home is in America
all across the Land of the Free
Home of the Brave
we gather in city after city after city
because we can
Tumbling Twin Towers
cannot keep us apart
though other forces did for decades

Home is in Australia
my sister
sends me her love
through cyberspace

Home is in Bangkok
my brother feeds me
gives me shelter for the night
we dine at the North Korean restaurant
end the evening at a room salon

Home is in Korea
in a candlelit garden
we gather to remember a brother
we never met
yet around the world
we celebrate his life
that ended too soon

In Korea, home is on the soccer field
where German, French, Italian, Danish, English,
mispronounced and misunderstood Korean
mix with the dust from our cleats

Home is in thirty countries on four continents
no matter that our Korean tongues
are now twisted like pretzels
we can no longer communicate with each other
much less pronounce each other's names
we are bound by a tie
we did not choose
but cannot be broken

So wherever you are
my brothers and sisters
Mattias, Dominique, Jos, Charlotte,
Bree, Susan, Jeff, Suryoon, Sang
my dongsaengs
my oppas, my unnis
wherever you are
that is home

What Do You Miss About Korea?

thank you T. S. for starting this conversation and J. C. for
continuing it

I miss being the majority
Koreans asking me for directions
hoping I never got anyone lost
I miss five dollar bibimbap
gathering at bars with silly names
like Hippo Hof
bad, cheap food
miles of tables
I miss mega city convenience
public transportation
gifted tailors on my block
Asian film fests
hiking with strangers
mountaintop soju toasts
Sunday soccer in four languages
coffee shops that star in Korean dramas
my stylist, VIP head spa treatments
twenty-four-hour beauty shops & restaurants
shooting ranges with coffee shops

I miss doorbells on tables
with options: *water, bill, help*

I miss dinner tables with toilet paper
all-purpose paper product.

I miss Korean guys
who want to go out with me just because
I miss making fifty dollar/hour
as an English prostitute
tax free!

I miss buying earflap hats I don't need
keep me warm on cold January nights
I miss relaxing by the Han Gang
like I'm in the movie *Gwaemul, The River Monster*

I miss meeting my brothers, sisters from Europe, Australia, Canada
I miss crowded Korean streets
rush hour subway football
I watch Korean movies
to glimpse street scenery
so I miss this friend less.

After I Left

My heart began its million-year fast
late-night rendezvous unfound
peeks darkened street corners
final subway trains
eternal Saturday nights
drunken Seoulites fight snowy midnight taxis
find movie theaters
hair salons
twenty-four-hour speed ramen
noraebang, spas
until 5:30 a.m. trains
bring new days

My heart traveled Busan bullet trains
devoured beach film festivals
watched bad Korean movies
nondescript streets,
crooked, stone cobble alleys
corner markets glimpsed
simmering sundubu fogs glasses

My heart flew across the Han River
drank overpriced appetizers at The Havana Monkey
friends crowded plastic covered booths
dodged Psy's Gangnam hagwon students

My heart closed meditation eyes
Buddhist temples chant 3:00 a.m.
remember times kept alive
friends' laughter dines on Korean BBQ, gogi jip
smoky, poorly lit January street kitchens

My heart felt August cold air conditioners
monsoon flooded shoes
July sweat drenched heart memories
coming going friends
revolving subway doors

My heart's million-year fast
stays alive
after great-grandchildren hearts
awaken buried memories.

Dual Citizen

Reparations: compensation in money, material, labor, etc., payable to an individual for loss suffered during or as a result of war.

Honorary citizenship
insults me
dishonorable face slap
on your exported children
we entered this world
as your fellow citizen

Dishonorable discharge
from Korea
stripped me of my status
your daughter
your son
your legacy

You took six decades
to return my birthright
now a jigsaw puzzle
with more lost pieces
than the population of Seoul
Have you no shame?
dignity delayed
this better life you gave me
bans me from this dual honor

You gave us the keys to the city
we've unlocked closets full of lies
exposed them to the world
through Samsung phones
you created

Why isn't my Korean citizenship
neatly packaged
with language fluency
my family intact
Korean status
lifetime airfare
between my forced home
and the peninsula?

Dual citizenship
not reparations
can you ever repair
emotional damage
trauma
repay lifetime family loss?

V.

A Holocaust of Children

Death Should Not Inspire Me

time to leave for writing class
social media post paralyzes

Daniel Larson-Fine
DOB: 1992/1993
DOD: March 24, 2017
Age: 25
Korean
Died by suicide
Place of death: Bloomington, Minnesota

suicide hotline gone cold
we missed your five-finger warning
a thousand friends could not save you
from recording your funeral dirge
our regret surrounds your lonely soul

Jane Trybulski
DOB: May 16, 2002
DOD: April 30, 2017
Age: 14
Korean

Died by suicide
Place of death: Penfield, New York

age does not protect us
death does not discriminate
countless lives abbreviated
mountains of names
enough to fill the King James Bible

Gabe Proctor
DOB: April 29, 1990
DOD: May 20, 2017
Age: 27
Adoption date: 2000
All American track athlete
Ethiopian
Died by suicide
Place of death: Lyndonville, Vermont

So Sorry floods obituary comments
digital condolences can't resuscitate
we pray peace and comfort
welcome you
our brothers and sisters
who left before you
will catch you on the other side

Phillip Clay
DOB: December 30, 1974
DOD: May 21, 2017
Age: 42
Adoption date: 1983

Adoption agency: Holt
Korean
Did not receive US citizenship
Died by suicide
Date of deportation to Korea: 2012
Place of death: Seoul, South Korea
Place of burial: Pennsylvania

strangers mourn your tragic death
Korean Consulate surrounded by grief
candle lit dusk hides tears

we expect death
for every life taken by suicide
how many more considered
this journey
from this life we cannot escape?
faces never match names
tongues won't count to five
in mother tongues

Did you choose death?
or did it choose you?
if we're four times more likely
to die by suicide
then is suicide
a natural cause of death?
when we're four times more likely
to die by suicide?

Open Letter to the Korean Red Cross

Dear Korean Red Cross,

Our commendations
four thousand family reunions
between North, South
vigilance, innovation
connects families face to face
letters, videos
seventy-five thousand families
wait since 1953
sober reunions
fleeting moments
sorrowful hellogoodbyes

No trace, effort
to reunify two hundred thousand families
Korean War divided
South Koreans
between East, West
two hundred thousand families ignored
waiting since 1953
Korean language lost
sabotaged reunions
negligence
switched children
tampered DNA tests

You shall be charged
with war crimes
civilian property destroyed
birth records lost
foreigners took us hostage

When do two hundred thousand ignored
East/West reunions begin?
we die every day
convoys of planes
travel West to East
without hope
we wait
please respond
before we're extinct

KADalicious

after Bao Phi, "FOBulous"

Kimchi As Delicacy
K9s Are Delicious
Korea After Dark
Korean Ajummas Dancing
Karaoke Ain't Difficult when you practice everyday
Korean Amazing Dramas
Kpop And DDR
Korean wave Always Drowning

Korean American Dream
Koreatown Always Developing
Koreans Are Dope
Korean Alcohol Drinkers
Korean Air Deals

Koreans Always Demonstrating
Korean Augmentation Army Division
Korean Allies Destroy
Korean Army Destroyed
Korea Already Divided
Kicking At the DMZ

Korean Agencies Dumping children in the west
Daily Adopting Koreans

Korean Agencies Deceiving
Korea Always Disrespecting adoptees
Killing Adoptees Daily
Korean Adoptees Dying by suicide
Korean Adoptees Dead
Korean And Dead

The Plane to France

Traffics unwilling Korean babies
descends on new white families
infant screams approved
for colonization

smiles beg university students
philosophy professors
research history
uncover ugly lies
better life minus kimchi

The Plane to Korea
gathers continents at baggage claim
hotel lobbies host unknown reunions
language borders trade stories

inter-continental couples
drink Hongdae basement clubs
consummate Sinchon hourly hotels
morning after pills
can't erase last night's fantasy
DNA tests find siblings
one night stand child
nephewniece

Pyeongchang 2018 Charter

The enjoyment of the rights and freedoms set forth in this Olympic Charter shall be secured without discrimination of any kind, such as race, color, sex, sexual orientation, language, religion, political or other opinion, national or social origin, property, birth or other status.
—Olympic Charter, Fundamental Principles
of Olympism, #6

Seoul 1988
Olympic stage set
Korea stands on world podium
humiliated
stripped of its gold medal
truth exposed
Korea welcomes Olympic world citizens
quietly ushers out 6,463 of its own
Babies for sale
South Koreans make them
Americans buy them

Let us not forget this human tragedy.
Let us not repeat this history.
Instead, let us uphold all humanity.
Let us honor all families
Single parents

Same gender parents
So that all children
will have equal opportunity
To learn
To grow up healthy, happy
To thrive in society
To serve their country through civic duty.

Let the thirtieth anniversary of the 1988 Seoul Olympics
mark the end of inter-country adoption
from South Korea
Let us usher in a new era
One that supports all unwed mothers
to raise their children
as they choose.
Let us not repeat our infamous history.

Korean ICA—Internment Camps
of Abduction

Thou shalt not be a victim. Thou shalt not be a perpetrator.
Above all, thou shalt not be a bystander.
—Holocaust Museum, Washington, DC

For over half a century we have called ICA
Inter-Country Adoption
international adoption
transnational adoption
a humanitarian gesture
love in action
building happy families
saving children
giving them a better life

Now we must call it what it is
this is a holocaust of children
this is a colonization of a people by their own
this is legalized child trafficking
this is cultural genocide
this is a violation of human rights
this is a war on bodies
this is a war crime
this is ICA
Internment Camps of Abduction

Korea, once occupied
now conducting your own occupation
you are occupying the lives
of two hundred thousand of your own
#10 OECD ranking
equals economic development and prosperity
postwar recovery
on the backs of your children
politicians sit
on their National Ass
profiting from yellow babies
bought and sold
on the open market
to the tune of
fifty million
US dollars in annual sales and profits
and when we return
you offer us
$200 in reparations

Mercedes, Lexus, BMWs
line Apgujeong Road
while boys and girls of all ages
line the walls of agencies
their destinations unknown
they wait for their numbers to be called
their prices to be named
their shipping dates to be set
your luxury cars cost more
than our $30,000 price tag
more precious to you

than these lives soon to be lost
you seethe with anger
at the sight
of a hairline scratch
on your 650i coupe
quietly breathe
a sigh of relief
as each shameful child leaves
this land
you dare to call a nation

This nation
this peninsula
is divided between north and south
No, this peninsula
is divided between east and west
every day
six
more
Korean families are divided
their babies abducted from them
sent to the internment camps
never to be seen again

Northwest Airlines? NWA?
NWA means Not Without Asians
Northwest refuses to leave Korea
without six Korean infant cargo
stashed away as commodity every day
their bankrupt business won't survive
without this international trade

University students sit stunned
as they learn the truth
of their national shame and guilt
yet remain divided
when asked to take a stand
it is no wonder
as we
have been deleted from history books
as you hope to erase generation
after generation
after generation of your unwanted people

You hoped
we would never return
you thought
you could hide the truth
but you can't hide us any longer
We are the history makers!
you are ashamed
that we have returned
and have marked our territory
yet you claim it as your rightful legacy
to celebrate an Olympic skier
you have taken one of our children
used him as your poster child
you've brainwashed and drafted us
to participate in your human trafficking
because it is legal you can do this with a sinful smirk

ROK—Republic of Korea? The ROK?
No! ROK means Rid of Koreans
rid of the unwanted people

who you refuse to claim as your own
children born to mothers
but not to fathers

Sent to the internment camps
you made us leave everything behind
our names
our language
our families
our heritage

Reclaiming our lives
you do everything possible
to make it impossible
for us to ever take back
what you
have stolen
from us
Japan stole your Korean names
now you
have done the same
and worse
to us
history does repeat itself

If these words are too angry
too militant for you
if they cause you discomfort
and you squirm in your seat
then I say
they are not angry enough
they are not militant enough

until you cannot sleep at night
and will take a stand
against
this
injustice!

North of the 38th or Mr. Obama
Please Apologize!

North Korea
the DPRK
Democratic People's Republic of Korea
Buk Chosun
a nation misunderstood
misrepresented
by mainstream media, politicians

A United Nations member for over two decades
this wounded animal
publicly skewered
on the axis of evil
an outpost of tyranny
quietly removed
from the US of A's terrorism list

North Koreans
long for reunification
peace on the peninsula
a strong, prosperous nation
One Korea: no North, no South, no East, no West!

North Korean Soldiers
protect us at the DMZ
the more peaceful side of the 38th parallel

North Koreans
the first Koreans to accept me
despite my background
refusing to sell their children
to white westerners
caring for their own
from cradle to grave

1866: the General Sherman attacked Korea but was destroyed

1968: USS Pueblo spy ship, captured
the first time the US government apologized
to another nation

Between these histories
lies the worst incursion of them all
the worst
because of its horrific intensity
the worst
because of its secrecy
never rectified
no resolution between the DPRK and the US
1950: the Korean War begins
the US invades Korea

Sinchon, North Korea
over thirty-eight thousand Korean civilians
women, children
massacred by US military in fifty-two days
mass murdered in churches
buried while breathing
butchered beyond recognition

two thousand people
pushed off the Soktang Bridge
mothers and children separated
burned after a petroleum bath

thirty-eight thousand killed
fifty days
Equals 25 percent of the population
Equals 738 per day
Equals thirty-seven per hour
Equals one Korean
every
two
minutes
Images from Auschwitz, Birkenau, Dachau,
Choeung Ek, Tuol Sleng surface as I check myself.
No, I am not in Poland
I am not in Germany
I am not in Cambodia
I am in Korea

Is this your Killing Fields, your Holocaust? I ask a survivor
It is worse he replies
as the painting of his tortured father
hangs in the Massacre Museum

Unexcavated mass graves
the Commission of the Women's
International Democratic Federation
finds these atrocities
surpass those committed
by the Hitlerite villains

Ugandan, Japanese brothers and sisters
fight for justice
Get out US army, Korea is for Koreans!

Lay flowers at graves of mothers, children
meet two survivors who escaped as boys
Jong Kun Song, age six
Ju Sang Won, age five
now grandfathers, museum guides
stand in the very place they were to die
recount the horrific event
some of the last survivors to testify this atrocity

Students wait to pay respect
our time too short
shouldn't we take more time to pay our respects?
no, then this infinite line of mourners cannot

Students stream through the museum
into the bunker, back out of the battery
who cared for the children who survived?
The state
The state gave them a place, status in society
valued them, cared for them
instead of selling them to white westerners
is this why the US cannot apologize
for this shameful history?

This history is not taught in US classrooms
it is not taught in South Korea
but it is taught tonight

Mr. Obama, Mrs. Clinton,
please rectify the past
apologize on behalf of your predecessors
and this country
you call the greatest nation in the world.
Yes You Can!

Teleporting Babies

Imagine a world
where Korean babies
could teleport
when white christian agencies abduct them
they can return
to their original families

What if their $30,000 purchase price
were invested
in a trust
in their name?
money would grow on ginkgo trees
liberate unwed mothers and their children
smash single mom stigma
take over National Assembly bedrooms

No need for twenty-week protests, impeachment
teleporting babies would have stopped
Pak Geun Hye voting booths
her father overthrown
into his Han River regime

Teleporting babies would rule
the Korean peninsula forever
kick out the US imperialist army
reunite north brothers and sisters

families divided between east and west
because teleporting babies
know what's best
for themselves
their people
the world

Teleporting babies know
stealing them from young, poor mothers
is not in their best interest
Teleporting babies
love everyone
not just the rich, powerful, white

Teleporting babies would rule
every continent
baby silence doesn't equal agreement
it means
we're planning our world domination
so love will dominate
so peace will dominate

Psalm for White Saviors

The white man is not my savior; surely I will be silenced in my
own family
He forces me to take his white name and pretend to be white
He takes me to church on Sundays, Wednesdays
strips me of my Korean heritage
He leads me on a journey of denial
Yea though I walk through the valley of assimilation
I fear death in my isolation
He blesses me with white privilege
only to take it away like a thief in the night
Surely I can't pass as white eternally
for my olive flesh, almond-shaped eyes
shall follow me all the days of my life
and I will dwell in my yellow body
with my white name forever.

My Ancestors Were Royalty

I come from a line of badass women
for only they had the grace
to spit in white supremacy soup

My lineage of women
never surrendered to saving face
quiet, demure stereotypes
submissive Asian females
we never caved to angry little Asian girls

My ancestors armed me
to shut you down
ignore your postured strut
insecure bullying

May my descendants know their royal blood line
flows purple like fields of mountaintop lavender
red, white and blue-swirled burgundy
cloaked in gold-trimmed velvet
platinum-clad, battle-ready

My ancestors taught me
having the last word
means to ignore yours

NOTES

Asian American History 101—The Summit refers to The APIA Spoken Word & Poetry Summit, a gathering of Asian Pacific Islander American (APIA) spoken word artists and poets.

How Often Do You Masturbate? was inspired by *not your fetish* by I was born with two tongues

Return to Sender—The Child Citizenship Act (CCA) of 2000 grants US citizenship to inter-country adoptees but is not inclusive of adoptees who were adults at that time. There are an estimated thirty-five thosuand adoptees living without US citizenship. Some have been deported and some of the deported have not survived. The Adoptee Citizenship Act aims to close this loophole.

Consider was written with the text of Scott Cohen's "Popular Turf Varieties," landscapingnetwork.com/lawns/types.html.

For My Mother is loosely based on *Things I Could Never Tell My Mother* by Denise Duhamel.

KADalicious—KAD is commonly used to refer to **K**orean **Ad**optee

Pyeongchang 2018 Charter—2018 will mark the thirtieth anniversary of the 1988 Seoul Olympics when South Korea's baby export business was exposed to the world and at which time South Korea greatly reduced the number of children being sent abroad.

Babies for sale. South Koreans make them, Americans buy them.
—Matthew Rothschild, The Progressive, January 1988

ACKNOWLEDGMENTS

It takes a village to make a poet. Let me introduce you to a few from my village.

"ASSIMILATION" was previously published in *Homeland Insecurities* and the *O.K.A.Y. (Overseas Korean Artists e-Yearbook), #5*. "For My Mother" was performed at the 2017 Listen To Your Mother show in Burbank, CA. "After I Left" was previously published as "After I Left Korea" in the *2017 City of Los Angeles Department of Cultural Affairs Asian Pacific American Heritage Month Calendar and Cultural Guide*. "Return to Sender" was previously published in *Cultural Weekly*, reprinted in *Portside* and included in the Arts + Advocacy: Citizenship for All Adoptees event at the Yerba Buena Center for the Arts.

Much gratitude to the team at Rare Bird! Thank you Tyson Cornell, Julia Callahan, and Alice Marsh-Elmer for reading my entire manuscript and venturing into the world of poetry! To the entire Rare Bird team—Hailie Johnson, Gregory Henry, Jake Levens, and Guy Intoci—thank you for bringing this book to life!

Love and eternal gratitude to *Mongrel*, The Asian Pacific Islander American (APIA) Spoken Word and Poetry Summit, Summit founders *I Was Born With Two Tongues* and *Isangmahal* and the 2011 Twin Cities Summit Organizing Committee. The Summit Family provided a space for me to connect with 1st generation and contemporary APIA poets and find my way through this jungle of a journey called life!

Thank you to the cofounders and founding members of Adoptee Solidarity Korea (ASK) in Seoul. You all are trailblazers and revolutionaries. You took an unpopular yet necessary stand on an important human rights issue and provided a space for me to voice my many conflicting thoughts and feelings on inter-country adoption that now live in these pages. We are nearly mission accomplished!

Adoptee Solidarity Korea – Los Angeles (ASK-LA), the Global Overseas Adoptees' Link (G.O.A.'L), the Dual Citizenship Planning Committee, and Koroot, your solidarity and commitment to equality and justice have weathered many a storm and continue to provide a light for generations to come.

Thank you to the many workshops and open-mics that nurtured my growth as a writer in Minnesota, Seoul and Los Angeles and all those from whom I've taken a workshop: Asian American Renaissance, Diaspora Flow, Equilibrium, Party Benefit & Jam, Our Mic, #90X90LA and Writ Large Press, The Poetry Lab in Long Beach, The Poetry Salon, The Anansi Writers' Workshop at The World Stage, Kaya Press, Studio Karimi, Rooftop Studios, the Allied Media Conference, and so many more.

Beau Sia, you made me stand on the ledge, literally. You helped me do the challenging work of owning and believing in My Words, My Life, My Voice. Thank you!

Jaha Zainabu, you are a model for any poet. I am blessed to know and learn from you!

Arianna Lady Basco, much appreciation for curating and editing a manuscript that sings. Thank you for pushing me out of my comfort zone in Our Mic's round #2.

Thank you Karen Gee for your expert legal advice!

Peace and love to AKoldPiece, Cynthia Allesandra Briano, Camari Carter-Hawkins, Jessica Ceballos, HyunJu Chappell, Jaye Cho, Jenna Cho, Chiwan Choi, Tammy Chu, Sharon Chung, Alexis Rhone Fancher, Angela Franklin, Cynthia Guardado, Andrea Gutierrez, David Hall, Robert Karimi, Nicole Kim, Annie Koh, Linda Kwon, Vincent Kuneen, Paul Mabon, David Mura and our virtual Asian American Writers class, Juliana Hu Pegues, Taia Perry, Bao Phi, Reverdia 'da River Woman, Siwaraya Rochanahusdin, Juyeon Rhee, Kim Stoker, Anne Sjogen, Natalia Sylvester, Kelly Grace Thomas, Suzanne Weerts, Dana Weiser, Tanya Wenning and Betsy Yoon. You and many more have played a role in my author journey from Minnesota to Seoul to Los Angeles!

Eternal love and peace to the late Joy De La Cruz and Brandon Lacy Campos. Your fire and light will always inspire me. Rest in Power!

Mil gracias to Las Dos Brujas Writers' Workshop and Chris Abani for the opportunity to learn in La Mision!

Last but indeed not least many thanks to Community Literature Initiative (CLI) and Founder & Director Professor Hiram Charles Sims. Your mission to make books and get us on the shelf made these pages a reality. This book would not exist without your passion for poetry and vision to make authors! Much gratitude and love to the CLI family. Special thanks to Year 3 Poetry and Extension, especially in naming my book!

ABOUT THE AUTHOR

Julayne Lee is an adopted Asian American poet, writer, artivist, producer, and sometimes blogger. Inspired and empowered by the Asian Pacific Islander American (APIA) spoken word groups Mongrel and I Was Born with Two Tongues, she began writing as a means of survival. Never intending to share her work, she realized after reading it publicly that as writing had brought her healing, it could do the same for others.

She has read in Seoul, Boston, Minneapolis, St. Paul, Berkeley, San Francisco, and Los Angeles. Julayne was selected for the 2017 Listen To Your Mother show in Burbank, CA. She has written for *Korean Quarterly* and her piece on the film *Casa de los Babys* was republished in *Uri Shinmun*, a multilingual publication based in the Netherlands. Her poetry has been published in *Homeland Insecurities* a chapbook fundraiser for the APIA Spoken Word and Poetry Summit, the O.K.A.Y. (Overseas Korean Artists e-Yearbook), #5, the 2017 City of Los Angeles Department of Cultural Affairs Asian Pacific American Heritage Month Calendar and Cultural Guide, Cultural Weekly and Portside. Her guest blog posts have appeared on *Land of Gazillion Adoptees*, *Slant Eye for the Round Eye* and the *Minneapolis–St. Paul StarTribune*. Julayne received a *Poets & Writers* grant for the Association of Korean Adoptees—San Francisco (AKA-SF) 20th Anniversary Reading with Poets and Authors. With a passion to amplify marginalized voices, she has produced and hosted readings and workshops for writers of color including Our Voices: A Reading & Discussion with Adoptees of Color as part of Writ Large Press's #90X90LA 2017. She has also spoken on adoption at symposiums and universities in Seoul and the US.

Julayne received her BS in Mathematics Education and has a Masters of Arts in Education. She is a co-founder and steering committee member of Adoptee Solidarity Korea—Los Angeles (ASK-LA) and served on the ASK (Seoul) steering committee. She is a Community Literature Initiative Scholar and a Las Dos Brujas Writers' Workshop alum.